Networking Ba

The Complete Guide on Network

Protocols and OSI Model. Includes

a Useful Section about Wireless

Home Networking

implied. Readers acknowledge that the author is not engaging in the rendering of legal, financial, medical or professional advice. The content within this book has been derived from various sources. Please consult a licensed professional before attempting any techniques outlined in this book.

By reading this document, the reader agrees that under no circumstances is the author responsible for any losses, direct or indirect, which are incurred as a result of the use of information contained within this document, including, but not limited to, — errors, omissions, or inaccuracies.

Table of Contents

Introduction

Congratulations on purchasing *Networking Basics,* and thank you for doing so.

The following chapters will discuss all of the different parts of your network that you need to know in order to set up the network and ensure that it is going to behave in the manner that you want. The goal of this guidebook is to help you learn some more about the OSI model as well, which can really help us to see how networks are going to behave, and what we are able to do with them as well. This guidebook will cover all of that, and more so you can be prepared with the results you get.

Learning about the different parts of networking is important, whether you are using a small network for your own personal use or if you are working with a larger network for your business or another use. Moreover, this guidebook is going to take the time to look at how we are able to handle this and what it all entails as well.

To start with this, we are going to look at some of the basics of wireless network technology. This allows us a chance to look at some of the technology that is behind our wireless networks, a look at some of the basics of home networks, and then compare and contrast the benefits and negatives of our wired or our wireless networks. We can then move on to some of the different network protocols that you can handle to ensure that our networks follow the different rules and regulations for the internet, and for some of the other communications that we need to focus on.

From there, it is time for us to dive a bit more into what the OSI model is all about. This is one of the main kinds of models that we can work with when it comes to networking and will ensure that our communications and connections are going to work the way that we want. The majority of this guidebook will spend time looking at the OSI model and how it works.

Once we have a good introduction to the OSI model and what it is all about, it is time to divide it up into some of the different layers that are present. We will look at the physical layer, the data link layer, the network, and the transport layer, allowing all of these to be explored individually so we can learn the parts that go with each one, and how we are able to utilize them for some of our needs.

The first four layers in this system are often thought of as one level of the OSI model, and that is why we will spend another section working on the last three layers of the OSI model, which will be the session, presentation, and application of the network and how all of these can be used to help us to get more done while maintaining the integrity and more on that network.

The final aspect that we are going to take a look at on our network to ensure we are able to use it well and get it all to match up well and secure is network security. This is the section where we are going to look at a few of the security measures that we need to know here, some of the importance of protecting our networks against cyberattacks, and so much more. The security of your network is going to be so important to make sure that no one is able to get onto the network and steal your information, and we will look at how to make this happen.

There are so many different aspects to the world of networking, and learning how to make this fit together, and a bit about the wireless technology that you have, and the OSI model will help us to start working with this process in no time. When you are ready to learn more about networking and what we are able to do with all of the models and the components of networking, make sure to check out this guidebook to help you get started.

There are plenty of books on this subject on the market, thanks again for choosing this one! Every effort was made to ensure it is full of as much useful information as possible; please enjoy it!

Chapter 1: The Basics of Wireless Network Technology

The first topic that we are going to look at in this guidebook is our wireless technology. This is a huge discipline within the world of IT because it is going to be one of the more affordable forms of networking. This is even truer when we talk about file sharing, access to some of the digital media that we want to focus on, and Internet surfing. With the rapidly growing mobile technology and mushrooming mobile device manufacturing, it is no doubt that this wireless networking is, and will continue to take the world years in, years out.

There have been many advancements in recent years when it comes to wireless. The most notable of these is the rise in all of the technologies that come with the word wireless. In this chapter, we are going to look at some of the different options that we can focus on when it comes to understanding this wireless technology and look at some of the essentials of the three most popular wireless technologies known as RFID, WiMAX, and Bluetooth. Let us look at how this works.

Wireless Hardware

It is important that before we get started, a wireless network, despite the name, is not going to be 100 percent wireless. There are going to be a variety of hardware components that will make this concept more of a reality. The following are going to be some of the most important out of the hardware components that we need to see in place before we are able to work on our wireless network at all:

1. Wireless NIC: The wireless network adapters are going to come with transmitters and receivers that are built-in. Once the adapters are installed within the devices that you want to work with, the devices are then able to transmit and receive the signals among themselves in order to reach the communication that they are looking for.

2. Wireless network router: This router is able to perform some of the conventional functions of a wired router. The biggest difference that we will see here is that the router for wireless is not going to be able to physically connect with some of the other network devices. Other than the function of packet forwarding, the router is going to be able to serve as the main access through which the users are able to connect to other networks and the internet. Devices are going to be served by the wireless router must have wireless network adapters.

3. Wireless Range Extenders: These are going to be the devices that are responsible for scaling the coverage of our wireless network. These are also going to be known as the range expanders or the boosters. The whole point of working with these is to make sure that they can amplify the signal and can make the quality of the signal a little bit better.

4. Wireless Access Points: These are going to be the wireless network devices that are going to act as the interconnection points. They are able to connect wireless clients to the internet, Ethernet, or some of the other access points that are all set up and ready to go.

SSID

To start with, the SSID is going to be the short form of the Serve Set Identifier. If we know that, in the context of our wireless technology, the service set is going to refer to a collection of wireless network devices, and then we should know that the SSID is going to refer to the technical name that identifies a given wireless network when needed.

Keep in mind that the SSID is going to be case sensitive and will hold onto up to 32 characters for the name. You can also work with some of the special characters in order to handle some of the SSIDs that we are going to see here. In addition to this, the Wi-Fi base, or the wireless router, is going to broadcast out this SSID, which will allow all of the devices that have Wi-Fin enabled on them to show a full list of the wireless networks that are within range.

An open network is just connected without us going through and trying to authenticate how it is going to work. Then we have the secured network, which is the one that most networks are going to rely on to keep things a bit safer and better to work with. These are going to request that the user or the device that wants to get on is able to provide a passkey. If they cannot, then this device is not allowed to get on.

Bluetooth

We also need to look at what Bluetooth is all about in all of this. To start with, Bluetooth came in as an alternative to the issue of heavy cabling that rocked the connection-based mobile phone, computer, fixed electronic device, and an assortment of hand-held device networking needs. This is going to be based on the 802.15 IEEE standard. Instead of using the cable to help transmit the data, it is going to work with the 2.4 GHz ISM frequency to help handle some of the transmissions that are going on.

The technology that is going to be used for Bluetooth will offer us the option of three power classes for the output of Bluetooth. The output power classes are going to determine the distance limits that are inside, and which data transmissions can occur as well. The three output power classes are going to include some of the following:

1. Power Class 1: The maximum output power that we are going to get with this kind of class is going to be 20dBm. The data transmission is going to be possible within an operating distance that is about 100m.

2. Power Class 2: The maximum output power that comes with this one is going to be 4dBm. Data transmission can occur within an operating distance of about 10m.

3. Power Class 3: The maximum output power that we are going to see with this class is going to be 0 dBm. The data transmission that happens here is going to go for about 1m.

This brings us to the idea of how Bluetooth technology is going to work. Enabling this kind of device is going to provide it with some of the power that is needed in order to search for any of the other devices that are enabled with Bluetooth within the data transmission range. An enabled device is going to employ an inquiry procedure to help discover some of the other devices that it will be able to reach and interact with as well.

Once another device that has Bluetooth discovers this device, it is going to work to relay an inquiry reply back to the Bluetooth device that started it all. What follows a successful inquiry reply is the entry of both deices into the paging procedure. In this paging process, the two devices are going to work in order to establish and then synchronize a connection. The completion of the establishment of a connection between these devices is going to result in what is known as a piconet.

The term of a piconet is going to be the ad hoc network that we want to focus on. This network is going to hold a maximum of eight devices that are enabled with Bluetooth. The device can comprise of different devices, but they all need to have Bluetooth enabled them to make it work. The devices can be many different types, including phones, mice, earpieces, computers, and anything else that is able to support the feature of Bluetooth.

Now, it is possible for us to go through and install this Bluetooth Network between the Mac OS X and any of the other devices that are enabled with Bluetooth on them. Some of the options that we are going to see with this one will include:

1. Click on Apple, and then go to "Systems Preferences."
2. Then we are able to click on Bluetooth and choose the Settings that are found under Hardware.
3. When we get that done, it is time to click on the button for Bluetooth Power on the window that is going to pop up to power the Bluetooth on.
4. To make sure that your Mac computer is set up to be seen by some of the other devices with Bluetooth that are within range, you want to click on the button for Discoverable.
5. You can then go through and choose the device that you want to connect with. This will have us select "Devices," and then we are able to choose "Set-up New Device." Then choose to Turn Bluetooth On in case it is not turned on in the first place.
6. After this is done, you will enter int the Bluetooth Setup Assistant, and it is going to provide you with the information that you need to go through and make the right selections with this.
7. There are going to be many options you can choose from, including the keyboard, another device, and mobile phones. We are going to work with Other Devices to make this happen.

8. The Bluetooth Device Setup is going to take some time now to begin searching for some of the other Bluetooth devices that are available and with which this computer will be able to set up the connection that it wants. When another device starts to show up, then a notification will show up on the screen. If you notice that this is the device that you want to work with, then select continue. This process is known as pairing.

The security that we have on our Bluetooth could require that we go through and provide a passkey. This is going to limit how many people are able to go through and establish a connection with that device. It is only allowable that someone with this passkey will be able to get onto that device and establish this kind of connection or link.

WiMAX

Another thing that we need to look at when we are doing some of our work here is known as WiMAX. This is actually going to stand for something, and the acronym is going to be used to help us break down how this works. To start with, WiMAX is going to stand for:

1. W: Worldwide
2. I: Interoperability
3. M: Microwave
4. AX: Access

This is going to be a kind of wireless broadband that was created to work as broadband wireless access. It was designed in order to help us handle some of our mobile needs and for fixed stations as a wireless alternative to last mil broadband access. It is going to be found in a frequency range of between 2 GH and 66GHz

The broadband wireless connectivity for some of the fixed network stations is able to go up to 30 miles if we need it. On the other hand, we will find that the frequency standards of this are going to be a bit different with about 5.8 GHz for the unlicensed part, and the 2.5 GHz for the unlicensed part.

In addition to some of the information that we are talking about above, there are going to be some investigations underway about whether we are able to use this technology to improve it to the 700 MHz frequency range, but this is something that we are able to look more at in the future.

Another thing to consider is the Orthogonal Frequency Multiplexing Division, or OFDM, which is going to be the format for signaling in the WiMAX. This format was chosen because it is going to provide us with enhanced non-line-of-sight, which is going to be known as NLOS, features that would help to get this all done in the right manner for us. This one is going o rely a lot on many frequencies in order to take a message and transmit it from the original source all the way to the destination. This is going to be even more important when we are working with things like multipath interference minimization issues along the way.

We are going to find that the WiMAX is going to be able to operate in both the multipoint and point-to-point arrangements. This is going to be very important when it comes to cases where the cable network and the DSL are both going to have access that is not available. This kind of technology for the wireless networks we use is going to be vital in the provision of last-mile connections. In addition, it is going to have a distance limit that can reach up to 30 miles if we need it.

Radio Frequency Identification

The next thing that we are going to look at is known as the Radio Frequency Identification, or the RFID. This is going to be one of the examples of the wireless network technologies available that will be employed mostly to help with the identification and the tracking of shipments, objects, persons, and animals using the radio waves.

The technique is based on the principle of the modulated backscatter. To keep this simple, the term of backscatter is going to refer to the reflection of the radio waves that are going to be able to strike our RFID tags. The radio waves ate going to reflect back to the transmitting source. The stored, inimitable identification information is contained in the reflected waves after it has reached this tag.

This kind of system is a great one to work with, but we have to remember that it is going to be made up of two main parts, including the RFID tag and the reader. We can remember also that the reader is going to be known as the transceiver in all of this. This is going to be made up of an antenna and a transceiver.

The transceiver that we work with, or the reader, is going to spend some time relaying radio waves that will be responsible for activating the RFID tag. This tag is then going to send back some of the modulated data, hopefully with the right unique information for identification back to the receiver. The transceiver is able to extract the modulated data that the tag of RFID sent in the first place.

There are three core characteristics that are going to be found in this kind of system, and they will include:

1. Frequency of operation.
2. This means that we will use it in order to power the RFID tag.
3. A protocol for communication that is going to be known as the interface protocol.

Let us first talk about the way that we are going to power our RFID tag. There are actually three types of classifications that we are going to see with these tags based on how they are going to gain the right power to operate. The three forms of these tags are going to be the active, the passive, and the semi-passive. Let us see what each one is going to be like.

First are the active tags. Batteries to ensure that they stay alive and that they will be able to do the right signal transmission back to our transceiver along the way have powered these tags. Then we have the semi-active tags that are going to be powered by the battery but will work with that backscatter principle that we talked about earlier in order to get the signals sent over to the reader. Then we end with the passive tags. These are going to use the rectification of the RF energy and will be able to strike the tag from the reader. This energy is going to provide us with enough power to keep the electronics on and the tag while sending back the right signal to the reader when it is needed

Using Wi-Fi to Extend Our Networks

Another thing that we are able to work with is how we can handle Wi-Fi and use this to extend the networks that we are creating. Most often, when you hear another person talking about wireless networking, they are going to refer back to the use of one or more standards of Wi-Fi. These are going to include the following standards, which are going to be found in many small offices and home offices:

1. 802.11g
2. 802.11b
3. 802.11n draft

These standards, when brought together and are going to be the standards that will allow our Ethernet networking to work without the wires. The standards are going to see some changes based on how they operate at the medium level. For the end-user, though, the most notable difference that is going to be found here is the speed. For example, the 802.11n standard is going to work with more than one radio transmitter and receiver to help speed up the process as well.

Although it is possible that the wireless networks are not going to completely replace the wired ones, they are still important because they provide us with consistent speeds of data, reliability, simplicity, and security. Some network implementations are going to eschew the use of the wires all together and will only rely on the connectivity of these wireless networks for the long term. Then there are some other implementations where the wireless networks are going to provide them with some of the supplemental connectivity.

In addition, it is possible to work with some of the WAPs that are going to be accessible to the public. These are going to be known as hot spots, and most of us have spent at least a little bit of time working with these at airports, hotels, coffee shops, fast-food restaurants, and more to help us stay in touch.

Understand the Security Threats

Before we end with this chapter, we need to look at some of the common security threats that are going to show up with these wireless networks. They are going to provide us with many great benefits, and they are a great option to work with, but there are a few issues with the security of the system that we need to focus on as well. Some of these are going to include:

1. Parking Lot attacks

Because the wireless signals are going to be dispersed from access points to some of the areas that they should not be, it means that these networks are going to be big prey for hackers and intruders if we are not careful. In this kind of attack, the intruder is simply going to hang around outside an organization in order to take advantage of that signal that goes beyond the perimeters of the company. This allows the hacker to really get into the network, gain access to some of the internal network resources, and cause some of the interference that they would like.

2. Shared Authentication Flaw

With this one, the hacker is able to go through and exploit some of the shared authentications that happens in a more passive attack. For example, they may decide to eavesdrop on the challenge when they want and then look at the response between the authenticating client and the access point. The hacker may choose to get ahold of the information for authentication and then use it in a manner to access the network. The best way to prevent this kind of issue is to encrypt all of the data that you are sending out between the access points and your clients.

3. Service set identifier flaw

Another option that we want to look at is the service set flaw. When the device that you are working with is not reconfigured, it is possible for the hacker to come in and use the default SSID to gain the access that they want to the network. It is important to do some configuration of the devices on the network in order to change up the SSID of that device and can help you to protect against this kind of attack.

4. The vulnerability of the WEP protocol

The good news is that WEP is not an option that a lot of programmers are working with any longer because they are not that secure and can leave a lo of your information at risk. However, when a wireless device enforces the WEP for security, they are more prone to eavesdropping because, on these devices,

WEP is going to be disabled as the default. This is why it is always a good idea to take the settings of the device and change them to meet your specific needs and try t change as much as possible so that the settings are not easy to predict.

There is a lot of information that we need to spend some of our time learning about and understanding when we work with these networks. It is important for us to be able to go through and learn more about how we can handle these and what we are able to do with them overall. Make sure to read this information and learn more about how to make these wireless networks behave in the proper manner for some of your own needs.

Chapter 2: The Different Network Protocols

Network protocols are the next important thing on our list to look at. These are going to refer back to some of the networking rules and regulations that are in place to assure efficiency in the functions of networking. These network services are going to be attainable thanks to the existence of some of these protocols on our networks as well. Moreover, the consistency that we need with some of these networking standards is going to be sustainable because we are using these protocols on the network.

Given the two different models that are used, it is very possible that we are going to encounter some dissimilarities in how these networking concepts are going to be implemented. This means that the implementation of the OSI and the TCP/IP network models is going to show us a lot of variation, especially when we are talking about some of the protocols of the network that will be applied. While the OSI network model is going to be discussed in more details through this guidebook, we are going to focus for a bit on the TCP/IP model

The TCP/IP Model

This is going to be a model that was developed first, much before we were able to look at the OSI model at all. This model is going to have four main layers that we are able to work with. These four layers, which are going to be listed from lowest to highest below include:

1. The network access
2. The internet
3. The transport
4. The application layers

There are going to be a few different types of protocols for the networks that are typical to each of the layers that we have above. Each of these is going to perform a specific role in order to contribute to the functionality of the layer that we are working with. The sum total of these functions will make sure that the network is able to complete its primary role of connecting together the devices sharing of resources, and making sure that the network is able to communicate in the right manner.

The Application Layer Protocols

This is going to be the first layer that we are going to see in this kind of model, and it is going to be known as the process layer in many cases. It is important because it will help us to handle some of the issues of representation and the high-level protocols that we want to focus on. This layer is going to permit the right interaction to show up between the user and the applications.

When this protocol in the application layer would like to have some kind of communication with one of the other application layers, it is going to send its message to the transport layer first. It is not possible to install all applications onto this application layer. It is only going to be the applications that are able to interact back with the communication system that we are able to add to this layer.

For example, a text-editor is something that we are able to install int his application, but if we are working with one of the web browsers that will work with the HTTP options, then we are able to place this into the application. The reason for this is that the browser is going to interact directly with the network. HTTP has to be noted in the protocol of the application layer.

There are a few other options that we are able to work with when it comes to some of the protocols that are important to all of this. Some of them are going to include:

1. SNMP: This is going to be known as the Simple Network Management Protocol. This will be the framework that we will work with to manage our devices on the internet. It is going to work with the protocol suite of TCP/IP.

2. SMTP: This is the Simple Mail Transfer Protocol. This is another protocol for TCP/IP that is going to support the services of email that we want to work on. The sending of messages from email to another is going to be possible thanks to this kind of protocol.

3. DNS: Domain Name System. This is going to be the connection of a host machine on the Internet that is going to be identified by the use of a unique IP address that is going to be assigned to each host.

4. FTP: This is going to be known as the File Transfer Protocol. This is going to be one of the standard internet protocols that we are able to use in order to transmit files in a network from the network on one of the machines over to another.

5. TELNET: This is going to be the Terminal Network. This protocol will establish a connection between our local machine and another remote machine so that the local terminal is going to be like a terminal at the remote.

The Transport Layer Protocols

This layer is going to be similar to the transport layer that we find in the OSI model. It is going to make sure that we see the end to end communication between the hosts. It is also going to have the responsibility of ensuring that the data is delivered without any errors. The transport layer is going to protect the application layer from any complexities of the data. In addition, there are a number of protocols that we are able to use in this layer as well.

The first protocol option that we are able to work with is the UDP or the User Datagram Protocol. This is going to be the cheaper alternative for the TCP. This protocol is not going to provide us with any of the features of TCP, which is going to make it less effective, but it is not going to have as much overhead, so it costs a bit less.

The UDP is going to be one of the best protocols that we are able to work with when we are in situations where reliable transport is not going to be the top priority that we work with. It is going to be the most cost-effective of all the options. It is also going to be a protocol that is connectionless, so we need to pay attention to it.

Then we are able to look at the TCP or the Transmission Control Protocol. This layer is going to ensure a reliable and error-free end to end communication, as we need between the hosts. This layer is going to help us to segment and sequence the data we are working with. In addition, this kind of transmission control protocol is going to come with a lot of valuable acknowledgment and will be able to control how the flow of data works thanks to the flow control mechanisms that are in place

While this is going to be a really effective layer to work with, it is going to carry a lot of overhead with it thanks to all of the features that show up with it. The more the overhead that we see though, the higher the implementation, so we need to keep this in mind as well.

The Internet Layer Protocols

The internet layer's functions are going to run parallel to the functions that we are going to see with the network layer of the OSI model. The protocol's definition occurs at the internet layer. These are going to be some of the protocols we need in order to handle the logical data transmission over the whole network. There are a few different types of protocols that we are able to work with when it comes to these including:

The IP Protocol. This is going to be the kind of protocol that we are able to use that is responsible for the delivery of the packets of data to the destination host from the destination host. This layer is going to help us by checking out the IP addresses that are found on the headers of the packets.

IP Is going to come with two main versions that we are able to focus on, and these will be the IPv4 or the IPv6. Most websites are going to rely on the former, but there is a growing number of places where we are going to see the latter as well. We are going to find that the IPv6 option is not going to be limited in number when it is time to handle the number of users.

ICMP or the Internet Control Message Protocol. This is going to be the protocol that we can use when it comes too encapsulated within the datagram. It is charged with the responsibility of the provision of information about the issues of the network to the hosts of the network as well.

Finally, we are going to see the ARP, which is going to be the Address Resolution Protocol. This is a protocol that is charged with helping us to figure out which host addresses are there using some of the ones that we are familiar with. There are a few options that are going to fit in with this, including the Proxy ARP, Inverse ARP, the Reverse ARP, and the Gratuitous ARP.

The Link Layer Protocols

The link-layer, which is often going to be known as the network access layer, is going to be a combination of the data link and the physical layer that we are going to see in the OSI model. This layer is there to help check out for the addressing of the hardware. The protocols that are found in this one are going to help our network to access some of the layer permits so that the data can be transmitted in a more physical manner.

First on the list is going to be the Ethernet Protocol. This is going to be one of the most widely used LAN technologies. The Ethernet protocols are going to operate themselves on the link layer of our TCP/IP network model, and it is going to rely on both the LLC, or Logical Link Control, and the MAC sub-layer of this as well. While the LLC is going to handle the communication that happens between the upper and the lower layers, the MAC part is going to handle the media access and the functions of data encapsulation as well.

Next is the Token Ring Protocol. This is going to be the protocol that will require our network topology goes through and defines the order that data should be transmitted by the host machines. All of the network hosts are going to be linked to one another with just one ring as well.

This kind of protocol is going to be important because it will use a token or a 3-byte frame that is able to move around the ring using the token passing kind of mechanism. Frames are also going to be able to move around this ring in the same direction that we see with this token to the right destinations as we go.

The FDDI protocol, or the Fiber Distributed Data Interface, is going to be another option. This is going to follow the standards of the ANSI and ISO that will help to govern how data can be transmitted on the fiber optic media in our LANs. Remember that these kinds of lines are going to have some restrictions with them and only go with a range of up to 124 miles overall.

This kind of protocol is going to work in a manner that is similar to the token ring protocol that we talked about before. FDDI is often going to be deployed as kind of the backbone that we are going to see with these WANs as well. There are going to be two main token rings that are found in the network. These two token rings are going to include:

1. The primary ring is going to provide us with a capacity that has 100 Mbps
2. The secondary ring that is there is a good backup to rely on in case the primary ring ends up failing along the way as well.

The Frame Relay Protocol

While we are looking at some of these protocols, we need to take some time to look at the Frame Relay Protocol. This is going to be one of the communication services that are packet-switched. It is going to run from the LANs to the WANs and backbone networks as well. There are going to be two main layers that we are going to be able to find with this one, including the physical layer and the data link layer.

This frame relay is going to be able to implement all of the protocols that are standard when we work with the physical layer, and it is often going to be applied at the data link layer as well. It is possible that the virtual circuits are going to be able to join one router to multiple networks remotely. Often, these circuits are going to make sure that the connectivity that we are working with reality. We can also choose to work with some of the switched circuits as well.

This kind of relay is going to be important because it is going to be based on the X.25 option, and it is going to be one of the fast packet technologies that we are able to work with. Data transmission is going to be done when we take our packets and encapsulate it into multiple sized frames. A lack of error-detection is the primary cause of how fast this is able to work with transmitting the data. Endpoints are going to be able to perform what is known as the error-correction functions, as well as some of the retransmissions of the drooped frames along the way as well.

There a few options that we can look at here when it comes to the frame relay devices. These are going to include the data circuiting terminating equipment and the data terminating equipment too. These are going to be important when we are taking a look at these network protocols in order to help us make sure that we are able to start it up and end it at the right times.

As we can see, there are many different types of protocols that we are able to focus on when it is time to work with some of the networking that you would like to accomplish. This networking is going to need these rules and regulations in place in order to make sure that it gets things done, that the computers and other devices are going to behave in the manner that you want and can communicate, and so much more. Take the time to look through all of these different types of protocols and see how well they are able to work for some of your needs along the way as well.

Chapter 3: The OSI Model

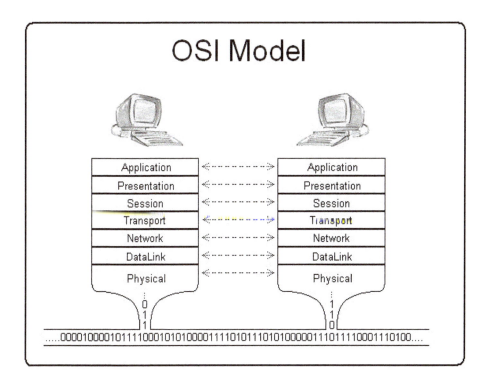

The next thing that we need to look at here is the OSI model. This is going to be a type of framework that will define the way that our device is able to communicate with the internet and the specific LAN that we are working with. We will find that this model, in particular, will be divided into seven separate layers, and each one is going to be independent of the others.

What this means for us is that it is possible that changes can occur over time. These changes, like improvement of performance and new protocols, can happen at each layer without really interfering with the functionality of the lower and the upper layer.

Remember that we said this model was going to have seven layers attached to it to make sure that it is able to work. The seven main layers that we are going to see with this one include:

1. Physical: The first layer is going to be where we find the raw bitstream is transmitted over the physical medium of our choice.
2. Datalink: This layer will help us to define what format the data on our network should be in. This is often going to depend on the kind of data that we use, and how the user is going to use this data as well.
3. Network: This is going to be the layer that helps us to decide which physical path we should give to the data we are working with.
4. Transport: This is going to be the layer where we see our data moved around and transmitted based on the protocols that are out there. The common protocols that are used for this are going to include UDP and TCP.

5. Session: This is going to be the layer that is responsible for maintaining some of the important connections and will be responsible for handling the sessions and the ports on the network.

6. Presentation: This is going to be the layer that will make sure that our data is in a format that is usable. It is also the place where we are going to see a good deal of data encryption happening as well.

7. Application: This is going to be the layer where the human to computer interaction is going to happen. The applications are able to access the services of the network in no time at all through this layer.

As we can see with this one, each of the layers that come with this model will be able to handle the job that is specific to them to make the network run, and it will be able to communicate with all of the layers that happen above and below it to ensure our networking behaves well.

Each of these is important to some of the work that we want to do in our projects, and we will take some time to go through each of them later. However, for now, we need to look at these in general and see how they are going to behave for some of our needs.

The OSI model is going to be there to help us understand, with as many details as possible, how our computer networks are going to work and can provide us with a better way to troubleshoot or solve problems that can occur in any kind of network, any of the events that will show up on our systems.

Each of the layers will help us to define how things will be able to operate in the communication of two or more devices, whether they are on the same network or not. Each layer of this model is going to come with its own protocols that, when they are combined, will be able to help us define how the network devices should behave.

For example, when we would like to be able to send some messages or traffic over to a specific server, then we need to know where to send this traffic or the destination. This means that we are going to work with the IP protocol. This is going to be part of the third layer of this method, the Network, which we will be able to talk about a little bit more later on.

There is another option that we are able to work with as well. This is where we would go through and request to download a file or to access a web page. When this happens, we are going to work with the different protocols that we see in these web pages, including the FTP or the HTTP.

To help us here, a protocol is going to be a set of rules that have to be met before we can do something on our network. That is all there is to it. It is going to be a set of rules of how these devices should behave on the particular network that you are using at the time. Most of the protocols that we concentrate on are going to be independent of one another. When we design things in this manner, and we can do that with the help of the OSI model, if there are changes to any of the protocols, it is not going to affect the others.

Now, we are going to spend some time looking at the specific options that come with the OSI model along the way. However, it is important to note that this is not a model that is all on its own. Some other options provide some competition for this model. The main one out there is the TCP/IP model, which was originally created and adopted faster.

This model is going to only come with four layers compared to the seven layers of OSI. In the first layer of the TCP/IP option, it is going to include the first two layers that we see with the OSI model, including the Physical and Data Link. Then, the last three layers of Application, Presentation, and Session are going to be just one layer when we look at the TCP/IP method and will be known as the Application layer.

The purpose of both of these models, though, is going to be similar, even though there are some changes. For example, both of these models are going to spend time allowing us to see communication between two or more devices, even when there are different applications on each one.

For example, if you are on a PC that would like to send out a request for the homepage of Google, it is going to start from the Application layer, the request being formatted in many streams of data, and it is going to move down the OSI model until it is able to reach the Physical layer. This is where it is going to be sent in the format of bits in this layer, as an electrical signal, light impulses, or as radio waves, all the way down the cable. This is going to be a process that we are able to refer back to as encapsulation.

Then the reverse is going to happen on the other end of things. This reverse process is going to happen when the request that we sent out to Google's web servers actually reaches that place. This would require us to go from the Physical Layer to the Application. Moreover, it is going to be known as decapsulation so that the whole process can finish.

This brings us to the question of why the OSI model is going to matter so much. While it is true that a lot of what we see with the modern internet is not going to strictly follow what is found in the OSI model because it follows the Internet Protocol suite instead, this model is going to be one of the best to rely on when it is time to troubleshoot any problems that happen on our network along the way.

Whether it is one person who is struggling to get their personal computer onto the internet, or there is a web site that has gone down for thousands of users, this model is going to be able to break down whatever problem we are dealing with at the time, and can isolate where the source of this trouble is showing up in the first place.

This is part of what is nice about the OSI model. It allows us to not only know about the problem but also figure out where the source of that problem is coming from. When we are able to narrow down the problem to just one of the layers of the model, we can avoid a lot of work that is not necessary, and even get the problem fixed in less time.

With that in mind, we need to look at how the data we work with on our network is able to flow through this OSI model. To make sure that we can take the information we have that is readable to humans and get it to be properly transferred over a network from one device to another one, we need to make sure that this data is able to go through all of the seven layers found in the OSI model in the sending device, and then travel up those seven layers on the receiving end as well.

We will take some time to explore the seven layers individually as we go through this guidebook, but we need to know that each one is going to be important and can provide our computer with some of the power that it needs, while properly handling some of the different parts of transmitting the messages that we want on that network.

Let us look at an example of how this is going to work. With this kind of system, we can suppose that Mr. Cooper is trying to send out an email to Ms. Palmer. Mr. Cooper spends some time composing that message in the application he has on his computer for emails and then will click on the send button. The email application that Mr. Cooper is working with is going to take that email and pass it over to the application layer that is able to pick out the protocol it wants to rely on, which is usually the SMTP before passing the data over to the presentation layer.

The presentation layer is going to be the part that is able to compress our data, so it is easier to move between the systems

46

before it is sent over to the session layer, which is going to be the step that is needed to initialize what is known as the communication session. The data is then going to head on over to the transportation layer for the sender, where it is going to be segmented. These segments can be broken up into individual packets while we are in the network layer, and then we can go to the data link layer that is going to break them down even more. The data link layer is going to take all of those parts of the code and deliver them over to the physical layer.

The physical layer is going to be important because it is going to take the time to convert the data into bitstreams of 1s and 0s and will send all of that out through the help of a physical medium, such as a cable. Once the computer for Ms. Palmer gets that bitstream that we worked on before, the data is going to head on through the layers that we just talked about, but it is going to be done in the opposite direction.

First, our physical layer is going to take the bitstreams out of the 1s and 0s and will put them into frames that we can pass to the network layer. Then the network layer is able to make the segments out of the packets before moving to the transport layer, which is the part that is going to take those segments and reassemble them into one big piece of data.

At this point, the data is then going to be able to flow over to the session layer of the receiver, which is the layer that is going to pass over that data to the presentation layer, and then it all will end with the communication session. The presentation layer removes all of the compression that we did before and will pass all of our raw data up to the application layer that we can use.

Finally, the application layer is going to be the point where we are able to feed the human-readable data over to the email server, which will allow her to read the email that Mr. Cooper sent to her on her own screen. This is a process that often sounds complicated, and it may have seemed through that explanation that it takes a long time. But it is something that can literally take seconds, if the network speeds are fast enough, and can really help us to better understand how networking and the communication on these networks, will behave.

Now that we know a bit more about the OSI model, we need to go through and learn a little bit more about how this model is going to work and what we are able to do to make it work for us as well.

Chapter 4: The OSI Model Layer 1 – Physical

Now it is time for us to go through and look at some of the different parts that are available with the OSI model. We are going to start out with the first layer that is known as a physical layer. When we work with this layer, it is going to specifically talk about the medium through which our devices are able to send out information. The main methods that we are able to use to connect networks and the devices we use to the network will include:

1. Electrical: This could include some of the UTP cables with 8 small copper wires.
2. Light signal: This is going to be the optical fiber.
3. Radio waves: This is going to be the wireless that we want to work with.

The physical layer is going to be the basis of our computer network because it will provide us with the physical connectivity that is going to show up between the networks and the various locations that are present. Each medium for transmission is going to come with some of their own advantages, but there are some disadvantages as well. For example, the advantages of wireless over the cable connections are something that we are really familiar with, including mobility and flexibility. However, we are going to find that there are some disadvantages as well, with the wireless network having issues with security and lower transfer speeds.

Instead of a cable connection, which is usually going to be a UTP cable, it is going to be more reliable and secure than a wireless network. It can help us to move around data at a much higher speed rate, and we are able to send them over a longer distance as well.

Another thing that we need to consider here is how we are able to transport some of the data that we want with the help of light. Here is where the optical fiber connections are going to come in, along with the signaling method, which is going to allow us to transport our data over a longer distance as well compared to the UTP cable. Moreover, usually, it is going to be done at a higher speed.

The UTP Cable Types

Now let us say that you want to go through and connect your laptop together with another one with the help of a cable. Things may seem like they are simple with this kind of situation. We can just take a cable and then plug it into our laptops, and it is all going to work fine, right? Well, there is a bit more that comes with all of this. For example, the UTP or the unshielded twisted pair, the cable is going to contain eight small wires. Out of these, four are going to be used to send things and four are going to be there to receive the traffics.

There are also going to be many device types, and each of them is going to require a different type of cable as well. For example, our PCs, laptops, access points, firewalls, switches, and routers are all going to work with a different type of code.

In addition, the UTP cable that we are working with is going to have two ends that we are able to plugin with the following methods:

1. Straight: These are going to be where we have wires that are the same at both ends.
2. Crossover: The wires are going to be crossed at both ends.
3. Rollover: The wires are going to be rolled over, such as what we find with the console cable.

Each of the devices that we listed out above is going to require one type of UTP cable when we try to connect it over to another device that is similar. These are going to help us to make sure that we are able to connect the devices that we would like. The straight cables are going to help us to connect together different types of devices, and then the crossover cable is going to be used when connecting some of the similar devices.

The Console Cable

The next type of cable that we are able to work with is known as the console cable. It is often known as the rollover cable as well. When it comes to accessing the router, through the command line, we are going to have two options. We can either connect it right to the port for the console, or we can do remote access with the help of the network by using telnet or SSH.

If we want to connect ourselves to the equipment, whether that is a switch or a router, through the console, then we need to make sure that we have the right physical access to the device. In most cases, this is not going to be possible. At first, when we are trying to set ourselves up from zero to a brand new network, we need to make sure that we are connecting over to the console port along the way. The reason we do this is that we are not going to come with an IP address on that equipment, to which we can remotely connect.

In addition, we have to remember that it is necessary to use the console port any time that we lose our access to the device. This can happen any time that something happens with the equipment or the network itself. This means that we need to go through and make sure that we troubleshoot and investigate what went wrong and how we can prevent that from happening in the future.

To help us go through and connect to any Cisco device through the console, we need to be able to work with a special cable that is known as the rollover. This type of cable is going to be inserted into a special port that is known as the console port. To help us connect to the Switch or the Router directly through the console, we also need a special program, something like SecureCRT, to make sure that we are able to get access to the command line of our switch or router to make all of this work.

Ports and Interfaces

Another thing that we need to look at is the ports and the interfaces in our network. A port is going to be the physical manner that we will use in order to connect to the network. This means that it is going to be the physical part and will be where we are able to plug our cables in. then we have the interface is going to be more about the logical part of our port, which is going to be the place where we are able to set our IP addresses from.

In the port, we are able to plug in the physical cable that we want to work with. On the interface, we are going to set up the IP address that we want to work with. For each of the ports that we work with, the speed is going to differ. It is possible to see this vary between 10 Mbps to 100 Gbps, depending on the model and the case that we are using. The current standard here in the LANs, at least at the user level, is going to be 1 Gbps.

It is also normal for the switches to come in with a higher port density. 52 is common here, but there are going to be some of the models that we want to work with that will have hundreds of these ports. This is because this kind of device is going to be designed in order to connect to more than one device that shows up in the same network.

The Full-Duplex and the Half-Duplex

We also need to look at another element that is important when it is time to look at how these ports work. Moreover, this is going to be a look at how the data is going to be sent over the network as well. The first one is the SW1 is able to send data by turn (the

PC sends, the Switch is able to only receive, and vice versa. When the switch is able to send it, then the PC receives, this process is not happening at the same time. When this happens, we are looking at what is known as the Half-Duplex. With this one, the devices are only able to send OR receive, but they cannot do them at the same time.

Then it is possible to look at the full-duplex option. This is when the SW1 is going to be able to send and receive the data that we are working with at the same time. This is going to be the full-duplex that we are able to work with. The main benefit of the full-duplex is that it is faster at transferring data networks that we would like to focus our attention on, but it sometimes depends on the kind of machine that we are working with and what our goals are in this process.

Collision Domains and Broadcast Domain

In any of the networks that we work with, a packet is going to help us to reach different points or conflicts with other packets that are transmitted at the same time. Here we will be talking about the broadcasts and the collision domains.

1. Collision domains

The first thing on the list to look at is the collision. This is going to refer back to the fact that there are two devices that will send a packet in the network, but they do it at the same time. If these packets are sent simultaneously, then it is going to form a collision. The reason for this is the way that the PCs and network devices used to work at the beginning of the Internet.

When the Internet was a brand new thing, devices were going to work in the way of the half-duplex that we just talked about. This means that a single device in the network was sending out traffic at a given time, while the other devices that were connected to that network had to wait for the first one to finish. When the first one was done, then it was easier to send out the traffic that was needed.

Of course, things have changed since that time, and we need to be able to have more computers, even in the same network, send out messages. A collision can only take place on a segment half-duplex from a network. Such collisions are not going to take place, or they will only occur in a rare manner due to errors because each of the devices transmits the traffic to full-duplex mode.

2. Broadcast domains

The next thing that we are going to work on here is the broadcast domain. This is going to be the distance that the packet is able to travel over the network. In other words, how far a broadcast packet is able to reach within the network will be the part that will represent the broadcast domain.

The first layer is going to be an important part when we take a look at the OSI method and how we are able to utilize it for some of our own needs along the way as well. The more that we are able to work with this network and get it to behave in the manner that we want, the better it will be for everyone. When we are done understanding how this first layer of the OSI method works, it is then time to move on to some of the next layers so we can see how all of them are going to come together and work well.

Chapter 5: The OSI Model Layer 2 – Data Link

The third part of the OSI model that we need to focus on is the Data-Link option. There are a lot of parts that are going to show up with this one, but we are going to take a look at the most important parts of this to help us understand how to work with this one a bit better and understand how we are able to utilize it for our needs as well.

The Basic Concepts of Switching

We need to start out here with a good look at what a switch is going to be all about. A switch is going to be a network device that is going to run at the 2nd layer of our model. The purpose of these switches is to interconnect more than one device to the same local area network as well. The reason that the switch is able to get all of this done is that it is going to contain more than one port that will allow the other devices that you want to work with to connect with a UTP cable.

Most of the switches that we are going to see will work with Ethernet technology. One of the reasons that Ethernet is so widespread is that it is a superior data and transfer speed along with bandwidth compared to the other technologies that are out there, especially considering what else is there when Ethernet first became available.

Ethernet is going to be very useful for us to work with because it will allow the Switch to have a good idea of where to send the data from one device over to another one. This is going to be based on the MAC addresses that we work with and the destination and source.

Remember here that the MAC address is something that we need to focus on because it is going to be the unique identifier that each device is going to have before it enters into a network. This address is going to be written out on the NIC of each of these devices by the vendor that made it in the first place.

How Can These Switches Learn the MAC Addresses

The whole purpose of working with one of these switches is that it is going to make sure that many devices are able to interconnect with one another in the same network. The way that this is going to be done is with the help of the MAC addresses on those computers. We will work with the address of the MAC destination so that it can be used to identify and then send out traffic to a device from the network. Then we have the source MAC address that is going to be able to store the port that the device is going to be located.

Therefore, looking at this in a practical manner, the Switch is able to go through and learn about each device that is on the network based on that MAC address, and then it is going to take some time to decide where it should send that information based on the destination MAC address that it has. This information is going to be stored in a special part of the memory that is known as the CAM table, or the Content Addressable Memory.

This table is cool because it is going to help hold onto all of the information that the switch needs about these MAC addresses, making it easier to open up and use the communication at any time that it is necessary to this process.

Outside of what we are going to find with our standard through the Ethernet, there will be a few other protocols and standards that we are able to work with when it comes to this layer of the OSI model. You could spend a lot of time working with them, but we are just going to mention them here, and you can decide which one of these will be needed. Some of the other protocols and standards that we are going to see that help us with this part of the OSI model will include:

1. The Point to Point Protocol or the PPP
2. Point to Point Protocol over Ethernet or the PPPoE. This is going to be used in many instances by ISPs for all of the great features of authentication that it is going to work with.
3. MPLS: This is going to be the current standard and protocol that is going to be found for organizations in order to make sure that they can connect their sites over to the ISP.
4. ATM or the Frame Relay. This is an older technology that we can focus on, but it is not really worked with as much as it was in the past.

Chapter 6: OSI Model Layer 3 – Network

Now it is time for us to move onto the third layer that we are going to see when it comes to the OSI Model. This is going to be a network. It is going to spend some time handling a few more parts of the whole thing that we are talking about above and can help us to make sure that our computer networks will behave the way that we would like. Let's dive in and see more about how this network layer is going to work, and all of the parts that are going to come together to make this one work.

Basic Concepts of Routing

The first thing to look at for this chapter or this layer is going to be the basic routing concepts. The MAC address that we talked about before is only going to be used when we would like to have some communication within the local network. For example, this address is only going to be used when there are two computers that are going to send traffic between one another on the same network. If these two would like to communicate online, then we would need to work with a router and an IP address to make it happen.

The purpose of working with this router is that it is able to come and connect multiple networks into a large network. This means that the main purpose of those routers is going to make a simple decision for every single packet that comes in.

By knowing some of the different network locations, it is possible for the router to go through and send the traffic from one of the networks to another. This is the process of moving the traffic forward towards the destination where you would like to send it. This is going to be known as routing. One thing to remember with this one is that with the default, the router is only going to know the networks that are directly connected.

This means that it is not going to have any idea on how to send the packets that you want further than those directly connected networks. This is where the administrators of this will come in. We have to go through and tell the Router which way to go so that our message and communication is going to reach the destination that we want.

When we first get that router to boot up, it is going to first take a few moments to learn about the networks that are directly connected. Making the routing process possible, the router we work with will need to work with the IP address of the destination as a reference point, and then the source IP address is going to turn into the source that we are going to work with.

TO help us to send out the packets or the traffic to the right destination, the router has to know a few things, but the very first thing is going to be the destination. This is going to be possible, but only if the Router learns how to reach that destination. This is a process that we are able to achieve in one of two ways, depending on what works the best for us. These include the Manual or dynamic methods.

Understanding the IPv4

The first kind of protocol that we need to look like is the IPv4. This was a protocol that was originally developed in the 1980s, and it was designed to work with 32 bits of data to help us to define an IP address. As you are able to see with the following example of 192.168.1.1, there are four fields that are going to be separated out by dots, and each field of these are going to be allocated with 8 bits of data as well. When we have 8 bits and multiply it by four fields, we are going to end up with 32 bits.

Now, we need to take a closer look at the number of bits that we have as well. This is going to tell us a bit more about the maximum amount of IP addresses that we are able to get out of this kind. This is going to be figured out by doing two to the 32 power. This will get us to 4.3 billion overall.

This means that we could end up with 4.3 billion of these kinds of addresses, and they would all be allocated to the right way. But why did we use the figure that we had above? This is because each bit can be either 0 to 1, so if we have 32 bits, we can generate about 4.3 billion of these unique addresses and numbers along the way.

It was during 2011, the IANA, or the Internet Assigned Numbers Authority to wend and allocated out the last of the address space for this kind of protocol. Does this mean that we are not able to connect to any of the other devices that we have on the Internet anymore? The good news is that this is not true at all. Since that time, there has been a lot of growth on the Internet since that time, and it is good news to know that we are able to utilize it still, even though the address space of the IPv4 will work.

One thing to note here is that there is going to be a big difference between what has been allocated and what is being used. IANA has provided out all of the IP addresses that it had available to the ISP, or Service Providers, throughout the world. However, this does not mean that the ISP has actually used all of these, or handed them all out to their customers along the way yet. There are still more of these out there that can be utilized as well in the future.

The maximum number of these kinds of addresses will be around 4.3 billion. However, in 2016, it was estimated that the total number of devices that were connected to the internet was around 20 billion. It does not take a lot of math to figure out that this is going to be a lot more than the number of IPv4 addresses that are available. Because of this problem, there have been some measures that were taken in order to slow down the allocation of these IPv4 addresses by using some of the different techniques out there, including NAT. it also introduced the idea of the Public and the Private IP. To another extent, another option that came out that was able to handle this problem, and which was able to handle some of these problems a bit better includes the IPv6 protocol.

The Structure of the IPv4 Packet

As we work with this one, there are going to be a few components that are important and that we are able to concentrate on when it comes to our IPv4 packets. Some of the ones that we are going to interact with the most in our IT studies and career will include:

1. The IP Source Address
2. Header Checksum
3. The Type of Service or ToS
4. Time to Live or TTL
5. IP Destination Address

We can take some time to look at these in more detail as we go through things, but we are going to start out with the IP addresses. We are going to have the destination address and the source address that we are able to focus on. In this case, we are going to reserve these fields for the destination IP and the source IP.

Then we have the IPv4 classes. There are going to be many fields that go with this one, but we can also spend some time dividing this into more than one class as well. Classes A, B, and C are going to be the ones that are used on the Internet. Then we can work with Class D as well. This is going to be the one that we will use for some of the multicast addresses, ad then we can work with Class E in order to work with some of the experimental stuff, and it will not be the stuff that we use that much.

We can also focus on the differences between the Private and the Public IPs that we can use. The Public IP addresses, as we can guess by their names, are going to be used in order to communicate the message over the Public Internet. Then we have the Private IP addresses that are going to be used more for some of the LANs that we talked about, including the ones for a school or a home network.

This means that when we are working with a private IP address of any kind, it is never going to end up reaching the Internet at all. For us to be able to work with the communications we want online; we need to work with the right protocol, such as a NAT, in order to handle the transforming of a private IP over to the public IP.

Ways to Send the Packets in Our Networks

There are going to be three main ways that we are able to send out some of the packets that we want in our network. Have you ever stopped to think about how the end-devices or the devices on our networks are going to send out the packets in that network? There are three main options that we are able to consider with this one including:

1. Unicast
2. Broadcast
3. Multicast.

When we look at the unicast mode, we will see that the communication that happens between the two devices is going to be one to one. This means that there is going to be a single source and a single destination. The best way to think about this unicast is similar to the manner that you talk to a friend, as you will just address yourself over to one other person.

Then we get the option of working with the multicast mode. This is going to be the type of communication that happens between devices that have one too many. This many is usually going to be to a specific group of devices. Imagine that you are in a room with a bunch of other people, and you are going to have a conversation with a group of about ten of those or a specific smaller group from the whole. This would be an example of how the multicast is going to work.

Finally, we are going to look at the broadcast mode. This is going to be the type of communication between devices where it is 1 to

n. this is going to be where the n is going to represent all of the devices that show up in the network. The Broadcast traffic is going to be the kind that is intended for every device that shows up in the network you are on.

We can go back to the previous example to help us out with this one. Imagine that you are in a room with 100 people again. In this case, though, you are going to be on the stage, and you will be able to share your message with all of the other people who are there. This is going to be the same thing that you will see when working with a broadcast.

The IPv6

Now that we have had a chance to look at some of the benefits, as well as some of the downfalls that come with the IPv4 option, we need to take it to the next level and look at what the IPv6 is all about. Think back to how we talked over the fact that there are over 20 billion devices that are connected to the Internet all around the world and that this number is continually growing. This is going to turn into a major problem, especially for ISPs because it is going to exceed, by quite a bit, the number of addresses that the IPv4 protocol was able to provide to us.

Therefore, this meant that there was a need for a better, and a much larger, type of protocol, and this ended up being IPv6. This is a new identification protocol that we are able to use that introduces to us a new address format, which is going to be hexadecimal, and a much, much larger addressing space than we are able to see with the previous example.

How big is all of this? The IPv6 is going to be 128 bits long. This means that we are going to have two to the 128th power of addresses that we are able to work with this one. This opens up a lot more availability in terms of the unique addresses that we need to be compared to the other option, and that helps to solve one of the major problems that we were facing before.

Outside of this feature, though, the IPv6 is going to streamline some of the processes of communication that happens with devices that get online, which is going to ensure that everything is faster and stays as secure as possible. One thing to remember with this one, though is that each of the IPv6 address fields is going to be separated out by the: symbol; there can also be a few exceptions that show up with this, such as the slash if it is needed.

We have to remember here that the IPv6 address is going to be a special one to work within the idea that it is only one that we can work with when it comes to the local area network or the LANs that we talked about before, in order to help communicate with other devices that are around. Remember here that these are going to be known as the local link, and it is going to be one that is automatically generated, which is another great feature that we see with the IPv6.

Working with these protocol options, especially the IPv4 and IPv6 is going to be important when it is time to handle some of the security and the other parts that come with our networking and will ensure that we are able to get this to work the way that we want in the process as well.

Chapter 7: OSI Model Layer 4 – Transport

The next layer that we are going to look at is the transport layer. This is going to be the layer that we need to look at to make sure any messages that we want to send through our network, whether it is to other computers on the network or it is to another computer throughout the world, you will find that this is going to be the layer that we need to take some time on. Let us dive in and look at the OSI layer 4 of Transport.

TCP

The first thing that we need to look at here is the Transmission Control Protocol or TCP. This is going to be a protocol that is going to do the exact thing that we think. It is set up to ensure the transmission of control of every single packet within the communication channel. We are able to find this along with the UDP on the 4th layer of this model, known as the Transport layer. As a Protocol Data Unit or PDU, the TCP is going to use segments to make it work. This means that it is going to be able to break down the data into some smaller segments that are easy to work with.

TCP is going to be a protocol that is already being used on many networks all of the time, even if you did not realize it was happening in the past. This is a good thing because it shows us how this protocol is doing a great job to keep all of the work seamless without interruptions. Think about when you do something like download one of the files that you need from the Internet, or you would like to access a web page, or even when you would like to connect yourself to a network device in any manner. When doing this, you will rely on the TCP protocol.

Now we end up with the question of why we need to work with the TCP. This is because the TCP is going to allow us a way to communicate by sharing the exact data, sometimes something as simple as a web page that the server or the client has access to. Therefore, when we go through the process of downloading a file through FTP, the TCP is going to ensure that all of the segments that compose a file that is located on the server will be received. In the case of segments that are missing, it is true that all of the work is going to be retransmitted.

There are a few benefits and features that we are going to enjoy from the TCP protocol and some of the many reasons why people would like to use this method over some of the others. These features and benefits are going to enjoy includes:

1. It is able to retransmit the data that we want to work with. This is true in the situation where it is being lost along the way as well.
2. Reordering the packet.
3. Establishing a connection between the server and the client, thanks to a 3-way handshake.

TCP is able to achieve all of the elements that we mentioned above with the help of a few message types, including PSH, RST, URG, FIN, ACK, and SYN. We are going to take a bit more time later on in order to talk about some of these message types as well.

Having all of the fields in the protocol header, you will find that the TCP protocol is able to provide us with many neat applications that we can utilize. Some of these will help us to reorder the data, retransmit the data in case the packet is lost with the help of the sequence numbers, and some reliable applications as well.

Each packet, or the group of packets we are working with, has a sequence number that we are able to associate with it. If the recipient is able to get a certain number of packets, defined by their own sequence number, then it is going to send back what is known as an ACK, or an acknowledgment message, for those packets when they are received.

This is going to make it easier for the recipient to take a look and figure out what packets have reached and which ones need to be retransmitted so that they go back to the person they need to reach. If the source, or the client, does not get the ACK for any of the packets, then it is going to take the time to retransmit those packets to ensure that it gets to the right location. At first, when the two devices are looking to communicate through a client-server connection, and then we need to start a session with a 3-way handshake to get it all up and running.

How Can Our Client Establish Its Connection to a Server?

As we mentioned earlier, when a server is able to communicate with a client, the two will be able to form a new connection between them. This connection is going to be important, and it will be known as the 3-way handshake. Now, we need to look at how this kind of handshake is going to happen and how we are able to utilize it for some of our needs as well. In the beginning, the client, which is going to be the computer who will start the connection, will send the server:

1. An SYN, or a synchronization message, marking the beginning of a session.
2. The server is going to respond with the acknowledgment or SYN-ACK.
3. The client is also going to respond to the server with the ACK, or the acknowledgment.

When we use this method, the TCP connection we are looking for, or the 3-way handshake, between the client and the server was then established for us to work with. Now, the two devices can help communicate with one another. This allows them to transfer files and send web traffic as well.

This mechanism is a great one to have on the network because it ensures that we are going to be able to really get the results that we want over the network. This mechanism of the 3-way handshake is going to help ensure the client and the server that all of the packets are being counted, or sequenced, ordered, and then verified at their destination and that nothing is getting lost along the way. Then, if some of the packets are found to be missing in this process, the sender is going to resend them so that the server is able to gather up all of the packets as well.

How Can We End This Connection?

After all of the packets have been sent over to the server, there is going to b a point when the connection is going to end. We do not need to go through and keep all of the connections that we create all of the time. This is going to cause many issues along the way, and there would be too much going on with the computer all of the time. We need to be able to go through and allow the TCP to terminate the connection for the best results. This is going to be similar to that 3-way handshake that we did above, but in this case, we are going to send out 4 packets. These steps are going to include:

1. The client is going to send out a FIN packet.
2. The server is then going to respond with their acknowledgment or the FIN-ACK.
3. The server is also going to send out a FIN message.
4. The client will then reply with the acknowledgment, which is the FIN-ACK.

When this is all done, the TCP connection is going to end between the two devices so that you can try another kind of communication with another system if you would like.

The User Datagram Protocol

The next thing on the list that we need to look at is the User Datagram Protocol. UDP is going to be the opposite of the TCP we just discussed, which means that it is not going to retransmit the packets, it is not going to establish a connection before it sends out the data, and it is not going to establish these packets at all.

Instead, the UDP is going to simply send out the packets from a specific source to a specific destination without having to take an interest in the status of the connection. The main benefit of working with this kind of protocol instead of TCP is that there is low latency. This is going to allow for a smooth transition of the application with the lowest delay possible.

The UDP is going to be suitable for many of the real-time applications that would like to reach the destination as quickly as possible. Because we are looking at some of the real-time applications, including CS Online, Facebook, and Skype, there are going to be a few requirements for Voice over IP, or VoIP, or other similar data sensitivity apps.

At the beginning of this chapter, we found that the TCP is going to use segments as the PDU, but when we are working with the protocol for UDP, things are going to be changed up. It is not going to use segments, but it is going to work with datagrams.

This means that it is going to break the data out into datagrams, which are going to be smaller in size so that we end up with segments.

Ports

In addition to the two protocols, that we are able to work with, it is important to look at something known as the ports. This port is going to be able to uniquely identify a network application, such as the DNS server and web servers, on a device in a network. Ach port has an identifier, which could be a number that ranges from 1 to 65535. When the PC is able to send out a request, such as what happens when we work with a web page, to the server, then this request is going to contain among others, the following kind of information including:

The Source IP: PC

Destination IP: Server

Source Pot: This one is going to be randomly generated through the Browser and will include 29813

Destination Port: 80

This means that with the information above, the PC's browser, with the source port of 29813, is going to make a request to the server, which is the Destination, and a web page, which is port 80.

All o these protocols and more are going to b able to come together in order to make sure that the ports and the protocols are going to behave in the manner that we would like. This takes some time to learn about and to get to work, but we have to make sure that this is going to match up the packets that we are sending between one computer to another.

There are many options that we are able to work with when it comes to a network, and we are going to be able to work with the communication between our computers and some of the different computers, whether they are on our network or on another network along the way. The TCP and the UDP protocols are going to be there to help us get things done and will ensure that the packets of data and information that are sent out will actually go to the locations where we want them.

The 3-way handshake that we spent some time talking about here is important because it is one of the best ways to not only make sure that the packets are going to end up in the end destination that we want. However, it will also spend some time making sure that our networks are safe and that no one is intercepting our data packets and messing with them. If a packet is not making its way through the network with the TCP protocol, we are going to be able to make sure that the packet will end up in its final destination where we would like it to be.

Chapter 8: OSI Model Layer 5, 6, and 7 – Session, Presentation, Application

So far, in this guidebook, we have taken the time to look through the first four layers that come with the OSI model. These are all going to be important to help with the communication and the connections that we will see when it comes to our network as well. Often the OSI model is going to be separated out into two parts. The first part will be the first four layers hat we already went through above. Then the second session is going to layer 5, 6, and 7 that we are going to talk about in this chapter.

Here, we are going to look at these three layers, which work closely with one another to give the results that we want here. We are going to look at these layers, which are known at the Session, Presentation, and Application layer. Let us get started with these three and learn what they mean to some of the networking that we are able to do with them.

Layer 5 or the Session Layer

The first layer that we are going to look at here is the Session Layer. This is going to be an important layer that is going to spend time creating, maintaining, and terminating the sessions between two of the network applications that you are focusing on. A session, which could be the communication between the two, is going to consist of exchanging a request to answer data flow between the two devices that are connected to the Internet.

In this system, the device that is requesting the data is going to be known as the client. This will help us to keep the different parts separate from one another. If you are the one that is making the request for the data in any connection, then you will be the client. However, the device that is able to provide the data is going to be known as the server. If you are getting a web page from online, you would be the client, and any device that is sending the web page over to you would be the server.

An important protocol that we will see with this layer is known as the LDAP, which is the Lightweight Directory Access Protocol. This is an important protocol because it is responsible for managing, searching, and modifying the directory service. This is going to include the place where all of the data on the user, like the passwords, user names, and other information on the user will be stored in this place.

With the help of this LDAP protocol, we are able to spend some time to exchange the user key elements in the network. Moreover, to be more precise, we are able to make sure that the session exchanges the network security process. There are other things that will show up in this one and we will notice that it is going to help with the User authorization and user authentication to finish up the process that we are working with.

Layer 6 or the Presentation Layer

Now that we know a bit more about the Session layer and what we are able to do with this, it is time for us to move on to the sixth layer of the OSI model, or the presentation layer. The purpose of working with this layer is to make sure the data is served up in the right format that is needed. There are a number of options that we can choose from here based on what data we are working with and what we are hoping to get out of the process. It could be something like PNG, JPEG, and JSON.

When we are working with this kind of layer, the data is going to be changed up and structured in a certain form, and then it is going to be delivered so that it can be interpreted on some of the applications that are based on the server. The types of formats that we are going to end up with here will depend on what we are trying to get out of the process as well. The data that you are storing and showing to the client will often dictate what you are going to save the data as.

A good example of this could be data encryption. This is important to the security of your network along the way. If you do not encrypt the data that you are sending from your network to another computer or even the data that you send to other computers to your network, you will end up with some issues along the way here. This just leaves the door wide open for a hacker to gain the access that they want to your network and so they are able to cause the issues that they want.

With encryption, we are able to go into the network and make sure that all of our messages are hidden and hard to find and read through. With a good amount of encryption, we are going to ensure that even if a hacker is able to gain access and take the messages, they will not be able to read it because the message will be a bunch of random letters and numbers until the right key is used. Since only the client will get the right key for this, the hacker will not be able to read what is going on.

The encrypted data, which is also known as the secured data, is going to be intended to hide some of the original content that we are working within another format that is harder to read through. When it is done in the right manner, we are going to find that it is possible to read the data and see what is there.

Layer 7 or the Application Layer

The final layer that we are going to take some time to look through is the Application layer. When we are using this context to talk about our applications, this means that we are just focusing on the network applications and nothing else. These network applications are going to be the ones that are offered by the server and could include some of the options that we want with things like remote access to a PC, email, and web application. Some of the protocols that we are able to get to work with this one will include:

1. HTTPS
2. SSH
3. DHCP
4. DNS

For example, when we are working with the HTTPS or the HyperText Transfer Protocol Secure, we are working with a protocol that is going to help us to access the websites that we want in the most secure manner possible. Some websites are not as secure, and they are going to rely on HTTP to help bring these. This one will only offer up the functionality that we are looking for, and nothing else.

Another protocol that we need to spend some time on here that will ensure we are able to access the internet and any of the websites that we want along the way is the Domain Name Services or DNS. This DNS is going to come in and take the domain name that we recognize and would use when doing a search of the website and can turn it into an IP address.

The reason that this is important is that all of the network devices are going to work with the IP addresses rather than the domain name. However, the user is not going to remember the string of numbers that go with all of the websites that they want to visit. This is why the DNS is going to be useful in order to handle all of this for us and will ensure that we are able to use the name that we are more familiar with here.

The Network Applications

Now that we have had a chance to go through and look at some of the different layers that complete the OSI model that we work with, it is time to take a look at a few of the applications. Below are a few of the different protocols that we are able to use, and the applications that our networks will use.

First, we are going to start with the HTTP protocol. This is going to be the kind of protocol that we are able to work with when it comes to traffic online. For example, the HTML files are able to transport from the server to the client when we would like.

There are a few other options that we can work with as well, including:

1. HTTPS: This is the same as the one above, but it is going to be a version that adds on some more security to the web traffic that we see.
2. FTP: This is going to be the protocol that we are able to work with that allows for some transfer of files between a server and its client.
3. DNS: This is going to be the tool that we can use to help find the IP address of our domain name.
4. Telnet: This is going to allow us a way to remote access a connection with our server or some kind of network device, whether it is a switch or a router.
5. SSH: This is going to be the option that allows us a secure way to work with remote access through our server or one of the network devices we talked about before.
6. DHCP: This is going to be the tool that is able to dynamically assign the IP addresses we need, and other information to all of the devices that are the end result of our   network.
   SMTP: This is going to be one of the mail transfer

protocols that we are able to work with and allows the different mail servers to work well with one another.

7. IMAP: This is going to be the protocol that we are able to use in order to transfer mail from the server to the client. You will find that the emails are going to be stored on this server.

8. POP3: This is going to be the option that we can use to transfer emails from the server to the client. We will find that these emails are going to be stored on the PC of the client with this one.

9. RDP: This one is going to allow us a way to connect remotely, using the GUI, to a macOS, Linux, or Windows Machine.

DHCP

One of the options that we need to look at here as well s the DHCP or the Dynamic Host Configuration Protocol. This is going to be one of the network protocols that is going to dynamically provide some of the different types of information that we need to the devices that we are able to connect to our network. Some of the information that we will find here includes the DNS Server, Default Gateway, and the IP Address and Mask.

The IP address is going to be able to help us to identify each device that is on the network, while the mask of the network is going to help us to determine the size and the range o the network. The DNS server is going to make sure that we can take the name of a website and translate it over to the IP address for that site. All of this information is going to be sent over to the server, though some of the smaller networks are going to send this through the Wireless Router.

That brings us to how this DHCP is going to work for us. When one of the end-devices, such as the smart TV, tablet, phone, or PC, connects over to the network, it is going to work to send out the Broadcast requests to all of the devices on the network. The point of doing this is to find the DHCP server that is able to provide it with the information we listed above. Some of the steps that we are going to see with this process include:

1. When the DHCP server or the Wi-Fi Router in some of the smaller home networks, see this message in the network, it is going to respond with the DHCP offer.
2. DHCP Offer: This is going to contain some of the information that the devices are looking for. Finally, the device is going to agree to the offer from the DHCP server

and then will send out a request for that offer to come on over.

3. DHCP Request: After the server is able to receive the messages, it is going to be able to respond back with the DHCP ACK.

4. DHCP ACK. This is the acknowledgment of the request that the device is going to provide back to the system.

Telnet

We can also look at the Telnet option. Telnet is going to be one of the protocols of a network that will allow us to remotely connect to a device on the network or to the server. It is a really widespread option to work with, and it is installed on a lot of devices that we use on a regular basis. We have to be aware that there are some big issues that can show up with using these as well.

To start, one of the biggest disadvantages that we are going to see with this is that the connection is not secure. All of the communications that happen with two devices that are working with Telnet will be sent out in the clear text, without the necessary encryption to keep it hidden, and this makes it easy for a hacker to come in and intercept the information that they want.

To help us to achieve the connectivity that we want, a program we can use with this includes PuTTY in Windows. With this tool, we are going to be able to connect ourselves to a device with the help of SSH, Telnet, and sometimes even through the console with a cable if we would like.

Telnet is going to be the protocol that will rely on port 23 in the TCP, and we are able to use it with any device, whether it works with Mac, Linux, or Windows. It is recommended not to use this, though since the traffic is not going to be encrypted and everything you send back and forth will be easy for someone to read through.

The Secure Shell or SSH

SSH is going to be a protocol we can work with that allows for some remote connections back to the network devices or the servers that we are working with. The connection is going to be better than we see with Telnet because it is going to be secure. With this method, both parties are going to take the time to encrypt the data so that it is harder, and sometimes impossible, for the hacker to get through.

For the most part, this is going to be the protocol that is the most widely used to help with some of that remote access because it is secure, and its flexibility is going to be built in from the beginning. SSH is going to work with port 22 on the TCP, and we are able to utilize it on any kind of device that we want, regardless of the operating system that is found on that.

Remote Desktop Protocol or RDP

Next on the list is the Remote Desktop Protocol or RDP. Because we took some time to talk about two protocols that will allow us to have a way to remotely access our network or our server devices, it is time to take a look at another protocol that is going to provide us with some of the same capabilities of accessing a device in a more remote manner but are going to work with the GUI, or graphical user interface instead. This is going to be a protocol that will provide us some good access to our laptop or our PC as needed.

As we can see, many different parts are going to come together when we are talking about the final of our seven layers in the OSI system. Knowing how these work and how we are able to benefit from them is going to be imperative to ensure that we are able to get the results that we want in the process.

No layer out of the OSI model is necessarily going to be stronger than one of the others, and none of them are going to carry any more importance than the others either. However, we will find that learning more about them and how each one is going to work can make a difference in the success that we will find with these layers and with the OSI model as well.

Chapter 9: Understanding the Security of Your Network

The next thing that we need to look at is known as network security. You will use your network for many different things. Whether it is the way that you connect to the world and share things, or you are more interested in just making sure that a group of computers is able to get along and share information with one another, you will find that the security is going to be very important for you to get these results.

It is probable that you will store a lot of information on the system that you work with, or on your network. Even as an individual, there are lots of parts to your network that you will likely want to keep private and hidden away or that you at least do not want to allow a hacker to gain access to along the way. This is where the idea of network security is going to come out and play.

You will quickly find that network security is one of the best things hats you can do for your network. If it is for your own individual network, then having this security is going to ensure that your emails, banking information, credit cards, and other information will stay safe. No network is too small for a hacker to go through and try to take the information that they can get.

The bigger networks are at risk for this as well. The hacker would have their choice of picking out a lot of information from these bigger companies to steal and use for their own. You could find a hacker go after the business itself and try to steal money and information from that company. Alternatively, it can go in the other direction and go after the customers who worked with your business over that time-stealing personal and financial information from the customers along the way.

No matter what is on your network, a hacker could potentially be interested in getting onto that network and stealing the information that they would like. Moreover, this is why we are going to spend some time looking at a bit of the importance of this network security and how we are able to use it for our own needs to keep our information and ourselves safe and secure.

To start, we need to look at what network security is all about. Network security is simply going to be the process of using physical, as well as software, security solutions in order to protect our network and all of the infrastructure that goes with it, from unauthorized access, malfunction, misuse, modification, destruction, or improper disclosure, The point of doing all of this is to make sure that the platform we are using our computer on is as safe and secure as possible.

Overall, this network security is going to spend time being concerned with the process of implementing security policies, tools, and procedures so that we can make sure that those who should not be on our systems, including people and programs, are not able to get onto that network. It can also prevent these attacks from connected devices and any of the data that is found in the traffic of that network.

Now, we have to keep in mind that network security is going to cover a variety of private and public computer networks that are used on a daily basis for us. From conducting transactions, communicating inside and outside of your company or government agencies, and even on an individual basis, it is important to rely on some form or another, and usually a strong form, of network security to get it all done.

The Basics of Network Security

The first thing that we are going to look at here when it comes to our network security is some of the basics that can help us out. Network security is a process that will start out with some authentication, commonly with the username or the password that you are able to set up for the network that you want to create. If we just work with the username and the password at this part, then this is going to be known as the one-factor authentication that we need.

This is usually pretty good, as long as you pick a username and a password that are hard to guess and that a hacker is not going to be able to get through with basic hacking means. Some of the networks that are more secure are going to work with authentication that will be two factored, or need two steps in order to be done. This is where the user will need to have contact with something, like their phone or some kind of security token in order to get onto the network along with their username and password.

In addition to this, there is the ability to work with three-factor authentication as well. This is usually reserved when we are talking about networks that are more complex and have a lot of important information in order to keep that information safe and away from those who should not access it. This one, in addition to some of the other steps, can work with a retinal scan, a fingerprint scan, or something else that is similar.

Once a user has gone through the authentication process, they should, the firewall that is in place is going to be able to enforce some of the policies in order to determined what is going to be accessible to the specific users on the network. Though the authentication is a great step to have in place to keep out those who should not be on the network, it is not perfect. It is often going to fail to check for worms and trojans that are transmitted over the network.

This is why it is common for the security of the network to come in three stages. All of these three stages are going to work together in a manner that provides us with a tired defense as well. These are going to include:

1. Protection Configuration of the systems and networks in order to get them away to function in the right manner with the control over the access.
2. Detection: This is going to be the ability to identify when the configuration has changed or when there is some traffic on the network that looks a bit suspicious.
3. Reaction: Once things have been identified, we are able to respond well to cyber threats and then will be able to return the network to a safe state as quickly as possible.

Cybercriminals will be able to work with multiple attack vectors in order to gain access to your network, so the defense in depth is going to be one of the most important steps that you are able to work with. You need to put in some security measures that are going to protect against different types of malicious software, such as malware, spyware, phishing, ransomware, trojans, and many other attacks online.

The good news is that if you are able to make your network security nice and tight, then it is a lot easier to go through and protect all of the data that is sensitive on your computer and can block some of the attacks. This is a great way to remove attackers before they are able to gain any kind of access to your network.

How to Implement Your Own Network Security

To help us go through the process of implementing a defense that works well for our network security strategy, we need to be able to work with a variety of different security controls that are going to limit the risks that your network will have online. Some of these are going to include:

First, we are able to look at administrative network protection. This is going to be a method of security that we are able to work with that will help to control the access and behavior of a network for the user. While it provides standard operating procedures for the officers of IT to execute any of the changes that are needed to the network along the way, it can ensure that everyone is only able to get ahold of the information that relates back to them.

We can also work with the antivirus and the anti-malware software that is on our network. These programs are there to help prevent, detect, and remove some of the malware that a hacker may try to put on your computer. Things like trojans, worms, and viruses can be sent to your computer and will try to spread through the networks. It is not uncommon for these to even stay dormant for a time in the machine that is infected, and these kinds of software can make sure that your network stays safe.

Application security is important as well. Applications that are not secure are going to be a big threat to the security o your network, and if you do not take care of it, it is common that attackers will try to gain some access to the network as well. The hacker can use a known vulnerability in the operating system or an application in order to enter into the network, and they can even send in viruses, malware, ransomware, and so much more.

Next on the list is going to be what is known as behavioral analytics. To help us to better detect some of the behaviors that are suspicious on the network, it is important to have a good understanding of what would be considered normal behavior.

Behavioral analytics and the tools that come with it will help us to flag activities that are suspicious automatically and can help your team to respond to some of the attacks that could happen.

Data loss prevention is going to be important in this whole process as well. Data loss prevention is something that our security teams are going to be worried about as well. We want to make sure that the staff who are dealing with this kind of information are not leaking that sensitive data, whether it is done intentionally or not. The DLP software that we are able to work with, along with some of the other measures of network security, can prevent others from uploading, printing, or even forwarding information that is sensitive to avoid some of the issues along the way.

We also have to make sure that we worry about our email security here. Email is going to be one of the biggest risks to cybersecurity that any company is going to need to worry about. Attackers are going to work with a variety of tasks here, including those of social engineering, in order to run some good phishing campaigns. If these are successful, it is going to allow the hacker to get their target over to compromised sites and can make it easier for the hacker to steal login credentials and even install malware on the computer.

Educating your staff about some of the different social engineering options that a hacker could try to work with, and going through some good measures to work on email security will be a great way to block attacks that are coming in. it is also a good way to control some of the outbound messages that employees and others are going to send out, preventing any sensitive data from being lost.

Next on the list is going to be the endpoint security. This is going to be a kind of methodology that we are able to use to help protect corporate networks when it is accessed through some of the remote devices that you want to work with, including our mobile phones and laptops.

Firewalls need to be in place on any network that is handling sensitive types of data. Firewalls are going to help us place an extra barrier between the internal network and any of the networks that we may not trust fully, such as the internet. They are going to work with this through a set of rules that are defined that are able to either allow or block traffic. We can work with both hardware, software, and sometimes a combination of both.

Honeypots are on the list as well. these are going to be some decoy resources on the network that are going to be deployed in the network as some tools that provide us with surveillance and some early warnings as well. These honeypots are not going to be accessed for legitimate purposes, so if you are able to access one, it is usually a good sign that we are dealing with a threat, and we need to deal with it soon.

IDS or intrusion detection systems. This is going to be a tool for network security that is meant to help us figure out some of the vulnerabilities that the hacker will want to exploit, malicious activity, and even violations to the policy of your network. It is going to make sure that we are keeping all of the policies in place that we want to work with, and can make our networks as safe and secure as possible.

Along the same lines are the IPS or the intrusion prevention systems. This is going to be the part that comes onto our network and will monitor for malicious activities. These could include security threats or violations of the policies that are in place. IPS is going to be able to identify any activity that is suspicious, look at the log information, such as the IP address and the hostname, and an attempt to block some of that activity if it looks bad before reporting it.

We also need to take the time to look at some of the security of our mobile devices and the security of our wireless networks as well. Like any of the devices we want to use, these wireless networks are going to come with some security flaws and vulnerabilities that could cause some issues. This, when it is paired together with the ability to connect to networks that are insecure outside of the office or when you are out, can increase the potential for some attacks that could come your way.

One of the most common types of attacks that are going to happen with these kinds of connections is the man in the middle attack. This allows the hacker to get right onto the network and intercept, or at least read, the information that is sent back and forth on the network as we do our work. It is important for us to take the time to train our staff and anyone else who is going to be on our network to only connect themselves when they are on a network that can be trusted.

NAC or network access control is the next part of this list. This is going to be the selective kind of restriction that happens on either a computer or a wireless network that we want to use. This process of network security is going to allow us to have control over who is allowed to be on the network and who is not.

When one of the users has the right permissions in place to get onto the network, then they will be considered an authorized user as well. With the right kind of control on who is able to get onto the network and who is not, you are able to prevent some of the unauthorized access while still allowing the right users to get onto the network in the way that they normally would.

We can also work with network segmentation. This kind of segmentation is going to help us to reduce some of the risks that we may be dealing with when it comes to network-based attacks spreading from the original computer all throughout the network. One of the common uses of this kind of segmentation is to make sure that we have an internal wireless network for the staff, and then a separate one for guests so that we can make sure that the spread of the attack is going to be limited as much as possible. We are able to split up the networks based on the location, roles, and more to ensure that the people we want on the network are able to get to the right parts.

Next are the security information and event management, which is known as SIEM. This is going to be able to bring together the information that your staff needs to help identify and then respond to some of the cyber threats that could become potential problems for you. These products are sometimes virtual and sometimes physical, and they can exist on servers and computers in most situations.

Technical network protection. This is going to be a kind of protection for our network that is going to be used in many cases to help keep our data safe inside of the network. The way that this is going to work is by guarding the stored and the in-transit data from any kind of software that is malicious and access that is not allowed to be there.

Along with the same idea, we are able to work with what is known as the physical network protection. This is the kind of protection we need for our network so that we can stop hackers from getting into the network components and interfering with it. Door locks, IDs, and swipe cards are going to be some of the most important parts of this kind of security and protection.

VPN's or virtual private networks are going to be the part that is able to encrypt the connection from an endpoint to the network that we find online on the internet. This is going to ensure that any of the staff that you work with and who are able to work remotely are able to securely connect to some of the internal resources when they are not in the office. Remote-access VPNs are often going to work with the SSL protocol in order to authenticate the connection between the device and the network and to keep it safe.

As we can see here, there are many different parts that we need to spend our time on in our network security. All of these parts are going to be important if you want to keep all of the data on your network safe and secure, and you want to ensure that no one is able to get onto the network and cause some issues or steal the information along the way. Make sure to work through all of these, and add them to your plan, in order to get the security of knowing that your network is nice and safe.

How Will Cloud Computing Affect Our Network Security

Many companies are moving to the cloud. This is a more efficient manner to take care of our network and will ensure that we are able to hold onto the information without needing to have all of the hardware and the resources that are needed to store this information. There are many benefits to working with the cloud for our business, but we need to look at how this cloud computing is able to affect the security of our networks.

The rise of the use of cloud computing is going to mean that a lot of companies are going to outsource their computing needs over to a variety of cloud service providers to make it easier. We have many options to work with when choosing our cloud service, but some of the most common and most popular options that we are able to work with include Microsoft Azure, Google Cloud Platform, and Amazon Web Services.

There are a few other companies out there who have some of the similar ideas to what we are talking about, but many of them are considering more of a hybrid approach to handling the computing needs we have. For example, many of these are going to focus on having their infrastructure behave party in the house, and then certain parts are going to be managed with the help of the cloud provider as well.

These cloud services are going to be some of the best ways to make sure that the company is able to increase their productivity, no matter the size of the company. However, we have to remember that when we work with these cloud services, there is the potential for some third-party and fourth-party risks. This is why the vendor risk management and third-party assessment frameworks are going to be some of the foundations when it comes to a strategy that includes cybersecurity for our needs.

When we work with these cloud services, we need to make sure that the control policies for security on that service are going to match up with the procedures and policies that your company is dealing with as well. This is going to ensure that your data is going to stay safe and secure. If you are not careful about looking into the security policies in place with the cloud service that you want to work with, then you are putting yourself at risk for a big data breach. Check into the S3 security that you are using, or someone else will.

Are There Different Software Options for Network Security?

There are going to be a few options when it comes to the software that we are able to handle so that our network security is going to behave in the manner that we want. To help us to handle all of the aspects of the security to our network, your company has to use a combination of hardware and software in most cases. Some of the options that you need to consider in order to handle this will include:

1. Web scanners
2. Firewalls that are based on web applications
3. Vulnerability scanners
4. Unified threat management solutions
5. Software that does a penetration test
6. Packet sniffers

7. Firewalls of all different parts, including the network and network segmentation.
8. Intrusion detection and prevention software.

We have to remember here that it is no longer enough for us to have a firewall set up and then call it good, assuming that we are going to be safe and not have any problems with the network security that we are working with as we go. Network security is going to require a lot more than this, relying on a defense that is more in-depth and we need to have it set up in a manner that is able to find and then stop some of the threats that are behind the firewall and in front of the firewall as well.

All of this is good, but we also need to go through and add in some good software that is able to automatically detect some of the vulnerabilities, the potential leaks of data, find the breaches, and the vendors that are at risk as well. This shows us that the security plan we have in place for our network is going to really need to come with many different parts, ensuring that no one who does not have the right access is able to get on your network and cause some issues as well.

The good news with this one, though is that there are many steps that we are able to work with when it comes to handling our network security and making sure that our data is going to stay as safe and secure as possible in this process. Some of the steps that we need to consider here include:

Be aware of social engineering and how it works. Social engineering is going to be the best friend of any hacker who is trying to get onto your system. They are going to love the ability to utilize this technique in order to get onto your system and cause some trouble. This method allows the hacker to get their victim to trust them. Whether it is a phone call that sounds official or an email that looks like it comes from a trusted source, the hacker is going to work to keep the victim playing along, at least until they get the information that they want.

Keep that antivirus, antimalware up, and running as much as you can. These are designed to help keep out some of the attacks that a hacker may try to do against you. If you update these and run a scan on a regular basis, they will ensure that trojans, malware, viruses, worms, and more are not able to get onto your system and compromise the network that you are using.

Do any of the updates that are necessary for any of your software programs and the operating system you use. Often there are going to be little errors or holes that show up in some of the software or operating systems that you use. When there is an update, this is a good way to fix those so that a hacker is less likely to get in.

Too many times, we are going to ignore these because we assume that they are not that big of a deal and that we do not need to work with them at all. However, if we forgo doing some of this, then we end up with operating systems that have vulnerabilities all over them, and we pretty much invite the hacker right in to cause the mischief that they would like. When a new update for an important software or for your operating system comes up, take the time to install it and do the update to keep the hacker out.

Do not give out personal information online to others. Whether it is through the emails, you get or a phone call or something else, you will find that keeping your information safe from those who ask for it is the best idea. Never assume that someone is who they say they are. In addition, never give out that information without being able to verify who is getting it in the first place.

Pick out strong and secure passwords, and do not use the same one on more than one account. Hackers have a whole host of tools that they are able to work with when they try to get ahold of the passwords to get onto accounts. In addition, if you choose the same password for all of your accounts, or you pick out a password that is not very strong, then the hacker is going to find it really easy to gain the access that they want as well.

It is important to pick out a strong password that is really unique. Do not go with something that relates back to you or something that is easy to guess. If it is a simple word in the dictionary, some dictionary attacks will hand that password over to the hacker in no time. Make sure that it is longer, has a good combination of letters and numbers, and is not really going to relate back to your personal life either. Moreover, always use different passwords for all of your accounts to make it even safer.

Double-check some of the websites that you would like to work with, and go straight to the website of the business that emails you. If you get an email from your bank or another similar company, rather than clicking on the link automatically, go to your search engine in order to get to that website. This will keep you safe and can make sure that the hacker is not going to be able to get your login information or any of the other data that is on your computer at the time.

Always watch out for some of the emails that you receive. Hackers like to get through to their targets through the internet.

This is because it allows them a way to go directly to the victim. Moreover, often, victims are not going to look that closely at the emails they get and will just click on the links that are there. We always need to double-check the information that we get online and through emails to make sure that we are not opening up something that is going to put us at risk.

Work with penetration and vulnerability testing to make sure that your network stays safe and secure. This is one of the best ways to ensure that we can find some of the areas that the hacker will try to get onto your system, and can give you some of the information that you need to keep them out. If you find some of these vulnerabilities, especially before a hacker does, you are able to go through and close them up ahead of time.

There are many things that we are able to do to make sure that our networks are safe and secure along the way. They take some effort on the way, but you will find that they are the best ways to keep the hackers out of your system, and will ensure that your data and your networks will stay safe and secure as well.

Conclusion

Thank you for making it through to the end of *Networking Basics*, let's hope it was informative and able to provide you with all of the tools you need to achieve your goals whatever they may be.

The next step is to look at some of the basics that come with networking, and what we are able to with is to help us to get the communication, the connections, and all of our work online and on our computers have done. There are so many parts of the network that we are able to work with, and this guidebook is designed to spend time looking at the networking basics that you need to know to get started.

This guidebook is going to spend a good amount of time taking a look at the OSI model and how this is going to work for some of the networking that you would like to accomplish. There are other methods and models that we are able to work with when it comes to networking and the proper protocols, but the OSI model is one of the most basic options, and the one that is the most effective, so a lot of individuals and companies want to spend their time with this one.

This guidebook took time to look at the basics of the OSI model, along with all of the different layers that are present with this model as well. We looked at all of the different layers, including the physical, data-link, network, transport, session, presentation, and application. All of these come together to help us to understand how networking will behave and what we are able to do with it to understand this process better.

In addition to looking at the various layers and steps that come with the OSI model, we also took some time to look at a few of the other parts that come with networking. We looked at the basics of networking and wireless networking, in particular, a look at how to keep your network security up and running, so hackers stay out, some of the important network protocols that can make a difference in your success, and so much more.

When all of this comes together, it is so much easier to create the network that you need, regardless of how you plan to work with this network in the first place. You will understand which protocols need to be in place, what layer you need to focus on for different kinds of problems and even some about how to keep the network safe from others.

Everyone can benefit from working with the process of networking in their life, and learning how to make it work, either for a business or a personal network, is always going to be a good idea. When you are ready to learn more about how to work with networking, and you want to work with all of the parts that come with it, make sure to check out this guidebook to help you get started.

Finally, if you found this book useful in any way, a review on Amazon is always appreciated!

ncontent.com/pod-product-compliance
urce LLC
· PA
080326
056B/1609